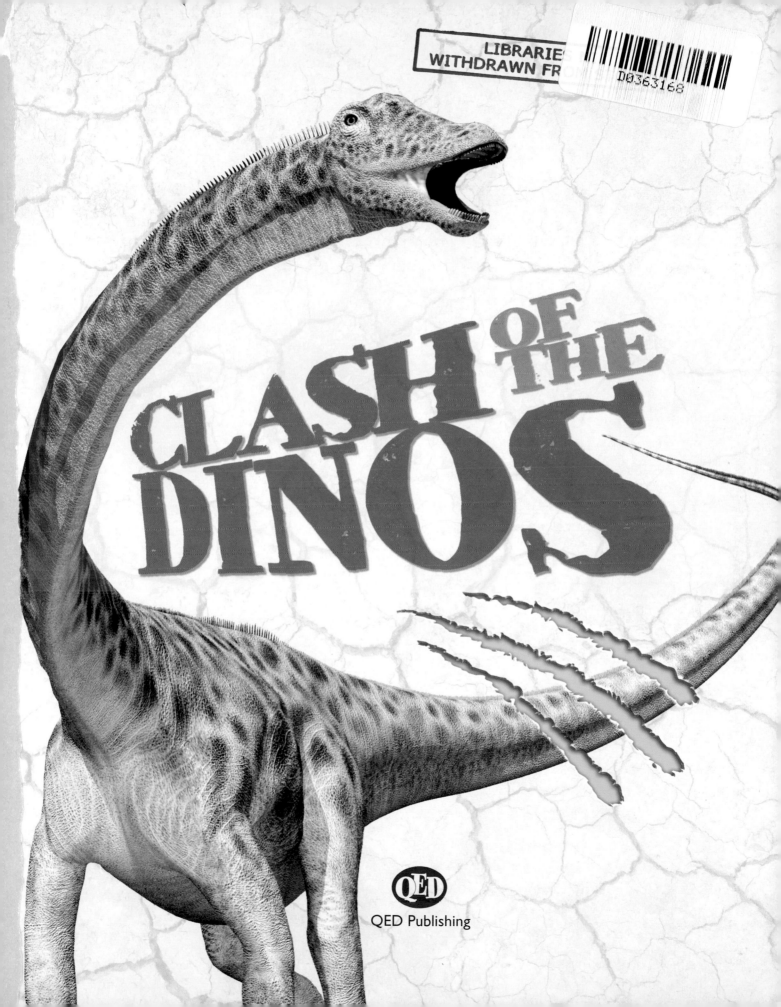

CLASH OF THE DINOS

QED

QED Publishing

QED Publishing, a Quarto Group company
The Old Brewery
6 Blundell Street
London N7 9BH

www.qed-publishing.co.uk

A catalogue record for this book
is available from the British Library.

ISBN 978 1 78171 681 6

Printed and bound in China
by 1010 Printing International Ltd

10 9 8 7 6 5 4 3 2

CONTENTS

4 .... Age of the Dinosaurs
6 .... Dinosaur Diversity

8–23 .... THE TRIASSIC PERIOD

10 .... Erythrosuchus vs Cynognathus
12 .... Euparkeria & Placodus
14 .... Special Skill: Flight
16 .... Herrerasaurus vs Saurosuchus
18 .... Desmatosuchus & Shonisaurus
20 .... Coelophysis vs Postosuchus
22 .... Eudimorphodon & Plateosaurus

24–37 .... THE JURASSIC PERIOD

26 .... Allosaurus vs Kentrosaurus
28 .... Diplodocus & Megalosaurus
30 .... Special Skill: Swimming
32 .... Ceratosaurus vs Brachiosaurus

34 .... Cryolophosaurus & Ophthalmosaurus
36 .... Battle Tactic: Speed

38–59 .... THE CRETACEOUS PERIOD

40 .... Deinonychus vs Tenontosaurus
42 .... Iguanodon & Kronosaurus
44 .... Battle Tactic: Armour
46 .... Pachycephalosaurus vs Pachycephalosaurus
48 .... Carnotaurus & Baryonyx
50 .... Battle Tactic: Agility
52 .... Tyrannosaurus vs Triceratops
54 .... Quetzalcoatlus & Velociraptor
56 .... Torosaurus & Mosasaurus
58 .... Special Skill: Herding

60 .... Glossary
62 .... Index
64 .... Credits

AGE OF THE DINOSAURS

Millions of years before the first humans evolved, life on Earth was dominated by dinosaurs and other amazing reptiles. Some fed on plants; others preyed on creatures smaller than themselves. The largest and fiercest took part in terrifying battles in a desperate bid to stay alive. In this book we look at the strengths and weaknesses of many of these animals, and how they might have fared when pitted against one another in a battle to the death.

EARLY REPTILES

The first reptiles appeared about 100 million years before dinosaurs. They evolved from amphibians, creatures like frogs and salamanders that spent part of their lives in water. Unlike the dinosaurs, which came later, the earliest reptiles were mostly small creatures, similar to lizards today.

Early reptiles: Hylonomus
The first reptiles belonged to a group called anapsids.

Flying reptiles: Pterandon
Pterosaurs evolved in the Late Triassic, 220 million years ago.

Mammal-like reptiles: Dicynodon
The first mammal-like reptiles lived some 300 million years ago.

Crocodiles: Teleosaurus
Lived at the same time as dinosaurs and have hardly changed to this day.

Turtles: Archelon
Triassic turtles, which are anapsids, appeared in the Late Triassic, 220 million years ago.

Lizards: Ardeosaurus
The first lizards lived in the mid-Jurassic, about 175 million years ago.

Ichthyosaurs: Stenopterygius
Ichthyosaurs were marine reptiles and were perfectly adapted to life in the sea.

MESOZOIC ERA

The Mesozoic Era was a time when many reptile groups evolved.
It stretched from about 251 million years ago to 65 million years ago.

TRIASSIC PERIOD

The Triassic period began about 251 million years ago and lasted until 200 million years ago. It was during this period that the first dinosaurs evolved.

At the beginning of the Triassic Period all of the world's land made up one supercontinent called **Pangaea**, which was at the equator. In this hot, dry environment the first dinosaurs thrived, while early mammals struggled to survive.

JURASSIC PERIOD

The Jurassic period began 200 million years ago and lasted until 146 million years ago.

Laurasia and Gondwana: During the Jurassic Period Pangaea broke into two landmasses – Laurasia in the north and Gondwana in the south. The climate became warm and wet and giant plant-eating sauropods evolved in a food-rich environment.

CRETACEOUS PERIOD

The Cretaceous period was from 146 to 65 million years ago. By its end, all of the dinosaurs had been wiped out in a mass extinction.

The Big Break: The world's land continued to break up during the Cretaceous until it looked similar to today's continents. The climate remained warm and wet which suited predatory beasts, such as Tyrannosaurus Rex, that ruled the land.

DINOSAUR DISCOVERIES

HOW FOSSILS FORM

We know about dinosaurs because of their fossils. A fossil is the remains of an animal or plant that has been preserved over millions of years, usually as rock. When a dinosaur died its soft parts rotted but its hard parts – such as bones and teeth – may have been saved if minerals seeped into them, and turned them to stone.

1 A dinosaur dies on a lakeshore.
2 The skeleton sinks into the lake.
3 Layers of mud settle over the skeleton, and the bones gradually turn to stone.

4 Erosion removes some of the rock above the fossilized skeleton.
5 As more rock erodes away, the skeleton is revealed.

DINOSAUR DIVERSITY

The biggest dinosaurs were more than 30 metres (100 feet) long and the largest creatures that ever walked the Earth. But not all were ferocious flesh-eating monsters. Many of the largest dinosaurs ate only plants. Others were light, speedy creatures only about the size of a chicken. We know there were at least 500 different kinds of dinosaurs, but there may have been many more that no one knows about yet.

WALKING TALL

One important feature of dinosaurs is the shape of their pelvis, or hipbones. It meant dinosaurs could walk with their legs directly below their body and straight, so they could walk and run in an energy-efficient and powerful way.

Dinosaur

Modern reptiles, such as lizards, have limbs that splay sideways, which gives them a sprawling posture.

Lizard

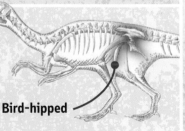

TYPES OF DINOSAUR

Dinosaurs are divided into two groups according to the shape of their hip bones. These groups are called the Ornithischians and the Saurischians, and both types evolved in the Late Triassic Period and died out at the end of the Cretaceous.

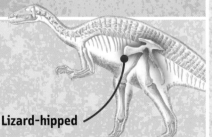

Ornithischians

Armoured dinosaurs
Stegosaurs
Boneheaded dinosaurs
Horned dinosaurs
Duckbilled dinosaurs
Iguanodons

Bird-hipped

Ornithischians ("bird-hips") had hips that were similar in shape to those of birds. This group included all plant-eaters, except prosauropods and sauropods.

Saurischians

Carnosaurs
Ornithomimids
Dromaeosaurs
Coelurosaurs
Sauropods

Lizard-hipped

Saurischians ("lizard-hips") had hips that were similar in shape to those of lizards. This group included meat-eaters (theropods) and giant plant-eaters such as Brachiosaurus.

BATTLE TACTICS

Score each dinosaur against its enemies using quick-reference categories of strength, armour, agility, scariness, special skills and speed.

STRENGTH
For the biggest dinosaurs, strength was a major weapon, whether for attacking prey or for defending themselves from enemies.

ARMOUR
Some dinosaurs and other reptiles had heavy body armour, made of plates of bone, as well as spikes and horns, which helped to protect them in battles with other animals.

AGILITY
Although many dinosaurs were lumbering creatures, others were amazingly agile, able to dart and leap as they attacked prey or defended themselves.

SCARINESS
Sheer size made many dinosaurs a terrifying sight. Even many much smaller reptiles were scary because of their sharp teeth and their ferocious fighting skills.

SPECIAL SKILLS
Many dinosaurs and other reptiles had particulary useful abilities, such as flight or a fantastic sense of smell or sight.

SPEED
Being able to move fast was sometimes even more important than being strong or well armoured – fast runners could escape from danger, or move quickly to capture prey.

DANGER LEVEL
Each animal is given an overall danger-level rating. This is the total of the scores for each battle tactic divided by six to give an average score.

EXTINCTION

Scientists believe that 66 million years ago an asteroid crashed to Earth in Mexico, creating what is now known as the Chixculub Crater. The asteroid was about 10 kilometres (6 miles) across and its impact had a devastating effect on Earth, causing a mass extinction event (a time when many species of animals and plants suddenly die out).

The impact of the asteroid was equivalent to thousands of nuclear bombs. Dust, ash and steam blocked out sunlight and dramatically changed the global climate. Many organisms – including dinosaurs – simply could not survive their changed circumstances.

SURVIVORS

After dinosaurs died out, the surviving mammals, birds and insects thrived and many new species evolved over the millennia that followed. The dinosaurs' descendants are still with us today as feathered birds, such as the hoatzin – which even resembles a flying dinosaur!

THE TRIASSIC PERIOD

The Triassic period began about 250 million years ago. The supercontinent, Pangaea, lay across the equator. There were no ice caps and the climate was very warm, with little change from season to season. Large areas of land were a long distance from the sea and so were drier than they are now, causing vast deserts. Flowering plants or grasses had not yet evolved, so the landscape looked very different from the world today, and there were vast forests of conifers, ginkgos and cycads. Huge ferns and horsetails also grew by lakes and rivers, and these were important foods for plant-eating reptiles, including the first dinosaurs.

Coelophysis

Morganucodon

Proterosuchus

Eudimorphodon

Plateosaurus

Placerias

ERYTHROSUCHUS
— VS —
CYNOGNATHUS

If this Erythrosuchus was just facing a single Cynognathus the battle would be quickly over, but fighting off a whole pack is a different matter. Taunted by the smaller animals, the Erythrosuchus must gather all its strength – and use its fearsome jaws, claws and tail – to slash, grab and wallop in every direction. Soon, the pack decides this fight is too risky, and retreats.

This Erythrosuchus has a massive head and a short neck. It just needs to wrap those jaws around one of its attackers, and the others may flee.

Erythrosuchus battle plan

This beast's name means "red crocodile" and, like its namesake, it had big jaws and cone-shaped teeth. Erythrosuchus probably had a good sense of smell, alerting it to the presence of dangerous enemies. It may have relied on speed and strength to kill its prey, munching down with great force.

ERYTHROSUCHUS

ORDER: Archosauria
FAMILY: Erythrosuchidae
PERIOD: Early Triassic
HOME TERRITORY: South Africa
HABITAT: Woodlands
SIZE: 4.5 m (15 ft) long

🔧 7	🏃 1	⚡ 3	☠ 7	★ 1	⏱ 4

DISTINGUISHING FEATURES
Erythrosuchus was one of the biggest and fiercest hunters on land at this time. With its large head and powerful body, it would have been a formidable enemy.

DANGER 3.8 LEVEL

WEAPONS OF WAR
ERYTHROSUCHUS   CYNOGNATHUS

- **Thick skin and powerful muscles** make this a formidable opponent.
- An enormous head with **huge jaws** gives this beast real bite force.
- Many **sharp, conical teeth** are perfect for gripping slippery prey.
- A **large body** means that only the bravest dare attack.

- **Pack power** – there is not just safety in numbers, there is strength too.
- **Dog-like teeth and jaws** can snap, grab, crunch and tear.
- Possibly **warm-blooded**, and that is good for speed and fast reactions.
- **Good hearing** is a real asset when you must remain alert to danger.

Cynognathus battle plan

This reptile had specialized teeth, just like modern-day carnivores such as cats – and they hunted in packs, like today's wolves. They may have worked as a team to find and attack their prey, using stabbing teeth to grab hold of flesh. Using pack power they could have pulled even large animals to the ground.

TIME: Early Triassic

THE BATTLE

WINNER: Erythrosuchus

CYNOGNATHUS

ORDER: Therapsida
FAMILY: Cynognathidae
PERIOD: Early Triassic

HOME TERRITORY: Argentina, Southern Africa, China, Antarctica
HABITAT: Woodlands
SIZE: 90 cm (3 ft) long

🔨 3	🗡 0	⚡ 6	☠ 3	★ 4	⏱ 6

DISTINGUISHING FEATURES

Cynognathus had a powerful body. Its strong jaws were lined with three types of teeth – for cutting meat, stabbing prey and chewing. This allowed it to deal with a varied diet.

DANGER
3.7
LEVEL

AGGRESSOR

EUPARKERIA

DANGER LEVEL **3.7**

EUPARKERIA LOOKED VERY LIKE a dinosaur but belonged to a group called archosaurs, or early ruling reptiles. Crocodiles and birds may be living archosaurian reptiles – crocodiles still look amazingly like their Triassic relatives.

 3

STRENGTH: Euparkeria was small but its jaws were remarkably powerful for its size.

🥷 3

ARMOUR: Euparkeria was lightly armoured with a row of bony plates, which ran down its back and tail.

⚡ 4

AGILITY: Euparkeria had a long tail, about half its body length, which helped balance its body when it ran on two legs.

DISTINGUISHING FEATURES
Like many of the dinosaurs that came later, Euparkeria's front legs were much shorter than its back legs. Its long jaws were studded with many long sharp teeth.

Class: Reptilia
Family: Euparkeriidae
Period: Early Triassic
Home territory: South Africa
Habitat: Dry plains
Size: 50 cm (20 in) long

☠ 3

SCARINESS: For an insect or other small creature, Euparkeria – with toothy jaws gaping – would have been a scary sight.

★ 3

SPECIAL SKILLS: Strong jaws and sharp teeth with serrated edges made this small dinosaur a successful predator. But it knew its limits and stuck to picking on creatures way smaller than itself!

⏱ 6

SPEED: A fast runner, this little reptile could also race along on two legs.

PLACODUS

PLACODUS, LIKE OTHER PLACODONTS, was happiest on seashores and swimming in shallow water rather than risking the open ocean. It fed on shellfish, which it prised from rocks with its specialized teeth.

4

STRENGTH: Massive muscles gave this reptile very powerful jaws and great bite power for attacking hard-shelled prey.

4

ARMOUR: A row of bony knobs along its back, and belly ribs on its underside would have made Placodus harder to crunch!

1

AGILITY: This reptile's body was too bulky for it to be agile either on land or in water.

Order: Placodontia
Family: Placodontlidae
Period: Early to Middle Triassic

Home territory: Europe
Habitat: Coasts and shallow seas
Size: 2 m (7 ft) long

DISTINGUISHING FEATURES
Placodus had a stocky body, short legs and long flattened tail that may have acted like a paddle for swimming power.

1

SCARINESS: Although it was a big animal, Placodus would not have frightened anything, except the unlucky shellfish it prised from rocks.

4

SPECIAL SKILLS: Placodus had an array of specialized teeth to help it gather its shellfish prey. At the front of its jaws were blunt teeth that stuck out and were used to pluck shellfish from rocks. Placodus then crushed its hard-shelled food with the broad back teeth.

3

SPEED: Placodus was not ideally shaped for aquatic life, but it did have webbed feet and a strong tail to help it swim.

SPECIAL SKILL FLIGHT

The first flying reptiles, pterosaurs, lived in the Late Triassic at the same time as the earliest dinosaurs. They were the first vertebrates (animals with backbones) to take to life in the air. There were at least 120 different kinds of pterosaurs but they were all extinct by the end of the Cretaceous. All had wings that were attached to the sides of the pterosaur's body and to the extra-long fourth finger on each hand.

RHAMPHORHYNCHUS

Rhamphorhynchus were the earliest, most primitive pterosaurs. They had short legs and a long, bony tail that made up about half the animal's length.

RHAMPHORHYNCHOIDS

The first pterosaurs were the rhamphorhynchoids and they appeared in the late Triassic. They had a large skull, toothed jaws, a short neck and a long, stiff tail. Most members of this group were extinct by the end of the Jurassic.

SCAPHOGNATHUS

Scientists think that this pterosaur may have had a much larger brain than most reptiles of its size. Perhaps its extra brainpower made it an especially good hunter. Its speedy flight would definitely have given it a head start over its prey.

PTERODAUSTRO

A pterosaur about the size of today's eagle, Pterodaustro soared over the oceans on its strong, yet delicate wings, searching for food to eat. Swooping down, it used its amazing jaws to scoop small prey from the water.

GLIDERS (MICRORAPTOR)

Microraptor was a small predator that measured around 40 centimetres (16 inches) in length. Feathers on arms, legs and tail formed wing-like surfaces large enough to generate lift and allowed it to glide. Curved claws on hands and feet suggest that Microraptor could climb, so it is likely that it launched itself from trees in pursuit of insects, gliding lizards and small birds.

PTERODACTYLOIDS

Pterodactyloids are the most familiar flying reptiles. They were similar to rhamphorhynchoids, but had shorter tails, longer necks and slimmer heads. Only a few types survived to the end of the Cretaceous.

PTERANODON

Pteranodons were massive, with a colossal wingspan of about 4 metres (13 feet). These airborne predators probably glided on warm currents, soaring over the ocean and scooping up fish in their toothless jaws and swallowing them whole.

PTEROSAUR SKELETON

A pterosaur's skeleton had to be light so it could fly. Many of its bones were very slender and some were hollow to lessen the weight even more. The long fourth finger of each hand helped to support the pterosaur's wings.

HERRERASAURUS
— VS —
SAUROSUCHUS

THIS IS A BATTLE of bulk versus speed and agility. Although the big-muscled Saurosuchus is the apex hunter of its day – it has no natural predators of its own – other, smaller animals might take their chances and launch an attack when surprise is on their side. The Herrerasaurus is part of a new breed of dinosaurs that are agile, not awkward – and quick, not lumbering.

Saurosuchus battle plan

Saurosuchus had size rather than speed on its side, and it would hope to overcome its prey with a mighty munch from its crushing jaws. Its plan might have been to bite hard once, then leave its opponent to bleed to death – before returning to feast on its meaty remains.

SAUROSUCHUS

CLASS: Reptilia
FAMILY: Rauisuchidae
PERIOD: Late Triassic

HOME TERRITORY: Argentina
HABITAT: Swamps
SIZE: 7 m (23 ft) long

🔨 6	🏃 1	⚡ 3	☠️ 7	★ 2	⏱️ 4

DISTINGUISHING FEATURES

A huge bite may be deadly, but it can leave a predator with broken teeth. Saurosuchus grew new teeth to replace lost or old ones, just like modern crocodiles.

DANGER
3.8
LEVEL

The Herrerasaurus has had a lucky break today. It has taken its bigger opponent by surprise, giving it a great advantage in a fight to the death.

Herrerasaurus battle plan

A powerfully-built early dinosaur, this predator ran fast, with its head facing forwards so it could keep its eyes on its prey. Its rear-facing, super-sharp teeth could sink into flesh, gripping and slicing it into mouth-sized chunks.

HERRERASAURUS

ORDER: Saurischia
FAMILY: Herrerasauridae
PERIOD: Late Triassic

HOME TERRITORY: Argentina
HABITAT: Woodlands and open spaces
SIZE: 4 m (13 ft) long

🔨 5	🏃 1	⚡ 6	☠ 3	★ 3	⏱ 6

DISTINGUISHING FEATURES

Herrerasaurus was about the size of today's largest lizard, the Komodo dragon of Indonesia. However, it could probably move much faster than its distant modern relative.

DANGER
4
LEVEL

WEAPONS OF WAR

Saurosuchus

- A **massive, deadly bite** can deliver the death blow in one mighty crunch.

- A **large, muscular body** and brute strength means this beast overpowers most opponents.

- A hunter benefits from **good eyesight** for judging distances.

Herrerasaurus

- Long jaws are equipped with many **sharp, rear-facing teeth**.

- Each forelimb had three **clawed fingers**, and two stubby fingers.

- A **long, whip-like tail** would give the animal better balance as it twists and turns at speed.

DESMATOSUCHUS

DANGER
4.2
LEVEL

THIS HEAVILY ARMOURED REPTILE may have looked fierce but in fact was a harmless plant-eater. A gentle giant, it was one of the largest animals of the Late Triassic.

4

STRENGTH: Big and powerful, this reptile had a strong, muscular body – but its jaws and teeth were surprisingly weak.

7

ARMOUR: Massive plates of bone protected Desmatosuchus's body, and a pair of spikes, up to 45 centimetres (17 inches) long, stuck out from its shoulders.

1

AGILITY: Its heavy body armour made it hard for this reptile to change direction or manoeuvre its body.

DISTINGUISHING FEATURES
This reptile's head was surprisingly small for its huge armour-plated body.

Order: Crurotarsi
Family: Stagonolepididae
Period: Late Triassic
Home territory: North America: Arizona, Utah, New Mexico
Habitat: All areas
Size: 4.5 m (15 ft) long

6

SCARINESS: With its sharp shoulder spikes, Desmatosuchus looked a lot fiercer than it really was. Fortunately many animals wouldn't venture close enough to find out.

6

SPECIAL SKILLS: Although slow-moving and docile, Desmatosuchus knew how to use its impressive bulk and body armour to maximum effect – by literally turning its back on its enemies!

1

SPEED: With its short legs and heavy body, Desmatosuchus could not move fast and depended on its body armour for protection.

SHONISAURUS

THIS OCEAN-GOING GIANT was a colossal beast and the largest of all the ichthyosaurs. With its sleek streamlined body, it could move up and down through the water, probably chasing squid to eat.

6

STRENGTH: A strong, powerful reptile, Shonisaurus had no equal in Triassic seas.

1

ARMOUR: Shonisaurus had no body armour, but its layers of blubber would have given it some protection from anything silly enough to attack.

6

AGILITY: Despite its size, Shonisaurus was very agile in the water, able to turn itself and steer with its paddle-like fins.

Order: Ichthyosauria
Family: Shonisauridae
Period: Late Triassic
Home territory: North America
Habitat: The seas
Size: 14 m (45 ft) long

DISTINGUISHING FEATURES
Shonisaurus had extremely long jaws, with teeth only at the front. The teeth were very sharp, allowing the ichthyosaur to seize hold of slippery prey.

5

SCARINESS: Sheer bulk made this ichthyosaur a very scary sight. No other creature would want to get in its way.

3

SPECIAL SKILLS: Shonisaurus was perfectly designed for life as a sea-living predator. An expert swimmer armed with sharp teeth, it could catch any prey it wanted.

6

SPEED: By using its powerful tail to propel itself forward, and its four flippers to move up and down in the water, this beast could move fast.

COELOPHYSIS
— VS —
POSTOSUCHUS

ONE OF THE EARLIEST DINOSAURS, Coelophysis is a fast-moving, merciless hunter. It seizes fish from Triassic rivers, and possibly gobbles up its own young. Packs may even work together to attack larger creatures. Postosuchus, however, is a heavily armoured, fearsome beast that is strong enough to attack dinosaurs even larger than a Coelophysis.

COELOPHYSIS

ORDER: Saurischia
FAMILY: Coelophysidae
PERIOD: Late Triassic

HOME TERRITORY: North America: Arizona, New Mexico
HABITAT: Forests, close to streams and lakes
SIZE: Up to 4.5 m (15 ft) long

🏋	1	🏃	0	⚡	8	☠	2	★	2	⏱	7

DISTINGUISHING FEATURES
One of the reasons Coelophysis was very quick and agile was that its leg bones were almost hollow and lightweight. This reduced the dinosaur's body weight and made it easier to move fast.

DANGER
3.3
LEVEL

A pack of Coelophysis could have done some damage to a large animal, but their best hope was to force a hungry Postosuchus to give up the fight and look for easier pickings elsewhere.

Coelophysis battle plan

Coelophysis was a fast, skilled predator that mostly hunted animals much smaller than itself. However, it might have attacked in packs, or worked together to defend the pack against larger predators – relentlessly stabbing with its claws and jabbing with its toothed jaws.

TIME: Late Triassic
THE BATTLE
WINNER: Postosuchus

POSTOSUCHUS

CLASS: Reptilia
FAMILY: Rauisuchidae
PERIOD: Late Triassic

HOME TERRITORY: USA – Arizona, New Mexico, Texas and North Carolina
HABITAT: Near swamps, lakes and rivers
SIZE: Up to 5 m (16 ft) long

| 🔨 5 | 🦎 5 | ⚡ 2 | ☠ 5 | ★ 3 | ⏱ 3 |

DISTINGUISHING FEATURES

The forelimbs of a Postosuchus appear to have been shorter than the hindlimbs, so it is possible that this beast walked on two legs rather than four.

DANGER
3.8
LEVEL

Postosuchus battle plan

A hungry Postosuchus lunged at a Coelophysis without realising that the pack was close by. Attacked from all sides, this mighty beast relied on its armoured skin for defence. It just had to wait for one of the lightweight dinosaurs to get a little bit closer to its dagger-like teeth ... snap!

WEAPONS OF WAR

Coelophysis

- The **long, flexible neck** allowed the head to move quickly.

- **Sharp-clawed fingers** can grab prey.

- Many **sharp, small teeth** were perfect for killing this predator's normal prey of fish and small animals.

- A **fast, agile, and lightweight body** means this was a swift hunter.

Postosuchus

- **Rows of bony plates** created a tough body armour for defence.

- The head was huge, with **long dagger-like teeth**.

- Its **size** meant this animal was invincible against all but the toughest enemies.

EUDIMORPHODON

ONE OF THE EARLIEST pterosaurs, Eudimorphodon was an expert hunter. This flying reptile soared over the sea, its large eyes always alert for any sign of its fish prey.

3

STRENGTH: Eudimorphodon had powerful wing muscles and strong jaws, but its body was small and light.

0

ARMOUR: Pterosaurs had no body armour and depended on their ability to fly swiftly away for protection.

7

AGILITY: Like all pterosaurs, Eudimorphodon was very agile in the air, able to swoop and dive and manoeuvre its body with ease.

DISTINGUISHING FEATURES
Eudimorphodon had a long bony tail that made up about half its total length. Its jaws were short, compared with those of later pterosaurs, and lined with two sorts of teeth – long peg-like teeth at the front, and short, broader teeth at the back.

Order: Pterosauria
Family: Eudimorphidontidae
Period: Late Triassic

Home territory: Europe, Greenland
Habitat: Open sea and coastal cliffs
Size: 100 cm (39 in) from wing-tip to wingtip, 60 cm (25 in) long

6

SCARINESS: With their big wings and gaping jaws, pterosaurs were awe-inspiring hunters.

7

SPECIAL SKILLS: Eudimorphodon probably flew low over the sea, keeping its highly effective eyes trained on the surface for any sign of prey. It would have held its long tail out behind it to balance its body in flight.

7

SPEED: In the air Eudimorphodon was a speedy, powerful flier. On land it moved more slowly, crawling on all fours with the help of the claws on its wings as well as its feet.

PLATEOSAURUS

A MASSIVE TAIL made up about half the length of this huge dinosaur. But good-natured Plateosaurus was a plant-eater and got no more daring than rearing up on two legs to munch the leaves of tall trees.

7

STRENGTH: Plateosaurus weighed about 4 tonnes and was a strong, muscular creature.

0

ARMOUR: This dinosaur had no body armour, but its bulk would have protected it from most other creatures.

2

AGILITY: Although it was not an agile creature, Plateosaurus was skilled at using its long tail to help balance its body when it stood on its two back legs to feed.

Order: Saurischia
Family: Plateosauridae
Period: Late Triassic
Home territory: Northern and Central Europe
Habitat: Forests
Size: Up to 10 m (33 ft) long

DISTINGUISHING FEATURES

Plateosaurus was one of the first huge plant-eating dinosaurs. Like many of the giants that came later, it had a long neck, small head and back legs that were longer than its front legs.

5

SCARINESS: When it reared up to its full height, Plateosaurus would have been an awe-inspiring animal, capable of scaring off many would-be predators.

1

SPECIAL SKILLS: Plateosaurus may have been an expert grazer, with little teeth and strong jaws for nibbling plants, but it was short of special skills for either attacking or defending.

1

SPEED: Plateosaurus was not a fast-moving animal. It usually lumbered along on all fours.

THE JURASSIC PERIOD

During the Jurassic, the world's climate was much warmer than it is now and there was lots of rain. These conditions were ideal for plant life, and large, dense forests of ferns, conifers and ginkgos grew over much of the land. So many plants meant plenty of food for plant-eaters, and more and more kinds of plant-eating dinosaurs evolved and flourished. These included huge sauropods, the biggest creatures that have ever lived on land. A sauropod could munch its way through more than 1 tonne of plants a day. Many different kinds of meat-eating dinosaurs thrived too, as they had lots of prey to choose from. Powerful killers such as Allosaurus, Megalosaurus and Gasosaurus prowled the forests, attacking anything that crossed their path.

Archaeopteryx

Allosaurus

Diplodocus

ALLOSAURUS — VS — KENTROSAURUS

THIS HUNGRY ALLOSAUR has been watching a herd of Kentrosauruses eating. At last, one strays away from the herd – and the Allosaurus strikes. As soon as the Kentrosaurus realizes what's happening, he bellows and pounds with his hooves. He lashes out with his heavy tail, cutting deep into his attacker's flesh. Despite her hunger, the Allosaurus retreats.

Allosaurus battle plan

The fearsome Allosaurus weighed up to 2.3 tonnes. As the largest carnosaur during the Late Jurassic period, it was more than a match for any animal of its time. These killers hunted in packs and even attacked huge sauropods and stegosaurs.

ALLOSAURUS

ORDER: Saurischia
FAMILY: Allosauridae
PERIOD: Early Jurassic

HOME TERRITORY: North America and Europe
HABITAT: Near rivers
SIZE: 12 m (39 ft) long

🔨 8 🗡 2 ⚡ 4 ☠ 9 ★ 4 ⏱ 5

DISTINGUISHING FEATURES
At 4.6 metres (15 feet) tall, the Allosaurus was a powerful animal. It had a number of openings in the bones of its skull. These were strengthened by a network of bony struts, giving lightness and flexibility to its massive head.

DANGER LEVEL **5.3**

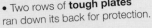

WEAPONS OF WAR
Allosaurus

- Dozens of very **large, serrated teeth** used like a hatchet to hack into prey.
- The ability to **open its jaw extra wide** to bite and devour prey.
- Powerful front legs, equipped with **long, sharp claws**.

Kentrosaurus

- Two rows of **tough plates** ran down its back for protection.
- Long, bony tail spikes that could **slash a predator's skin**.
- A **flexible tail** that could move quickly with great power to deliver a blow.

The Allosaurus was a great threat to smaller, plant-eating dinosaurs and may even have made a meal of heavily armoured ones.

TIME: Late Jurassic

THE BATTLE

WINNER: Kentrosaurus escapes

KENTROSAURUS

ORDER: Ornithischia
FAMILY: Stegosauridae
PERIOD: Late Jurassic

HOME TERRITORY: Tanzania, Africa
HABITAT: Forests
SIZE: 5 m (16 ft) long

🔨	4	🥋	8	⚡	1	☠	3	★	4	⏱	2

DISTINGUISHING FEATURES
The Kentrosaurus had a double row of armoured plates and spikes running down its back, with long spines on its tail to defend itself with.

DANGER
3.7
LEVEL

Kentrosaurus battle plan

With its tail spikes and bony plates, Kentrosaurus was a dangerous prospect for any predator. Only the largest flesh-eating dinosaurs, such as the Allosaurus, would dare attack anything from the Stegosaurus family. Kentrosaurus was a lumbering creature best left alone by all but the hungriest carnosaur.

DIPLODOCUS

EVEN FOR A DINOSAUR, Diplodocus was enormous, one of the largest animals that has ever lived. Longer than a line of seven average cars, this huge reptile weighed more than three African elephants.

9

STRENGTH: Just moving its own bulk demanded immense strength, so this dinosaur had extraordinarily powerful muscles.

0

ARMOUR: Although Diplodocus had no bony plates or spikes on its body, its huge size was protection enough from all but the fiercest and most foolhardy predators.

2

AGILITY: Despite its huge bulk, Diplodocus could rear up on its back legs to feed on high plants, using its strong tail as support.

Order: Saurischia
Family: Diplodocidae
Period: Late Jurassic
Home territory: North America
Habitat: Open plains
Size: 26 m (85 ft) long long

DISTINGUISHING FEATURES

Diplodocus had a huge body but a tiny head for its size. At just over 60 cm (24 inches) long, its head was not much bigger than the head of today's horse.

6

SCARINESS: Although this leaf-eating giant was not an aggressive animal, its size made it a terrifying sight for smaller dinosaurs.

5

SPECIAL SKILLS: Powerful muscles enabled Diplodocus to pound its hooves and lash its huge tail from side to side. This dramatic display would be enough to frighten away most predators.

1

SPEED: Diplodocus was not a fast mover – its massive pillar-like legs were designed to support its great bulk, not for speed. The dinosaur ambled along at about 6 km/h (4 mph), not much faster than most humans.

MEGALOSAURUS

DANGER
5
LEVEL

THIS HUGE, MEAT-EATING DINOSAUR was a killer, capable of attacking the great plant-eaters that roamed the same forests. Megalosaurus was the first dinosaur to be scientifically named, in England in 1824.

7

STRENGTH: Megalosaurus was a powerfully muscled animal with a big, strong body and tail, capable of tearing other dinosaurs limb from limb.

0

ARMOUR: This dinosaur had no body armour, but with its collection of weapons it had little need of protection.

5

AGILITY: Megalosaurus's heavy tail helped to balance its body as the dinosaur ran and pounced on prey. Walking on two legs allowed this dinosaur to move deftly.

DISTINGUISHING FEATURES
With its large head, powerful jaws and curving, serrated teeth, Megalosaurus was well equipped as a hunter and killer.

Order: Saurischia
Family: Megalosauridae
Period: Jurassic
Home territory: England, Europe
Habitat: Woodland
Size: 9 m (30 ft) long

7

SCARINESS: This killer was one of the scariest creatures of its time and, with its ability to kill dinosaurs twice its size, struck terror into the heart of any plant-eater.

5

SPECIAL SKILLS: As well as sharp teeth, Megalosaurus had strong clawed fingers and toes, which it used to grasp its prey and tear at its flesh.

6

SPEED: Megalosaurus walked upright on its strong back legs and could run at speed for short periods when chasing prey. It may have hidden in wait for its prey before swiftly pouncing.

SPECIAL SKILL SWIMMING

While dinosaurs ruled the land, marine reptiles dominated the oceans. There was a rich source of food in the seas and they quickly evolved to swim, hunt and fight for survival. Some – such as the ichthyosaurs – even developed a fish-like appearance. Plesiosaurs evolved flipper-like limbs and massive bodies.

PLESIOSAURS

Plesiosaurs had strong bodies, short tails and long flippers. They fed on fish and squid and spent nearly all their lives in the water. However, just like turtles today, plesiosaurs clambered onto land to lay their eggs.

ELASMOSAURUS

Elasmosaurus had the longest neck of all the plesiosaurs and it lived in the oceans during the late Cretaceous Period. These giants measured up to 14 metres (46 feet) long and hunted fish, squid and other small sea animals.

SKELETON OF A PLESIOSAUR

Scientists can tell how an animal moved by looking at its skeleton. The strong bones of a plesiosaur's chest and hips suggest that these animals had huge muscles and were powerful swimmers that beat their forelimbs (flippers) like wings to 'fly' through the water.

LIOPLEURODON

This deadly predator rivalled the size and strength of the greatest sauropods. At 20 metres (66 feet) long, Liopleurodon was one of the largest animals to ever live. Short-necked plesiosaurs – like Liopleurodon – are called pliosaurs.

PLACODONTS

Placodonts were amongst the first reptiles to adopt a marine lifestyle. They thrived in the Triassic, but had died out by the Jurassic. Placodonts were equally at home on the shore or in shallow water, searching for shellfish to eat.

HENODUS

The heavily-armoured Henodus is the only known placodont that lived in rivers or lagoons – all the others lived in the sea. It grew up to 1 metre (3 feet) long and looked similar to a turtle, with its tough 'shell', a beak-like mouth and four limbs for paddling through the water.

ICHTHYOSAURS

A typical ichthyosaur had a sleek, streamlined body with a strong tail that helped propel it through the water. Like dolphins today, they cruised the oceans at high speed, hunting any prey that came their way – mostly fish and squid. They did not come to land to lay eggs, but gave birth to their young in the water.

SKELETON OF AN ICHTHYOSAUR

The ichthyosaur's strong tail provided its main swimming power. The reptile beat its tail back and forth to push itself through the water and used its paddle-like front legs for steering. The plesiosaur swam more slowly, moving itself along with beats of its long flippers.

CERATOSAURUS
— VS —
BRACHIOSAURUS

A HERD OF BRACHIOSAURUS is feeding in the afternoon Sun. A lively youngster decides to explore and moves away from the herd. A big mistake. A pack of Ceratosauruses have been watching nearby — they pounce, clawing and biting at the Brachiosaurus's tough skin. The sauropod struggles bravely, lashing his tail and roaring. But his wounds are too deep and he soon dies. The Ceratosauruses enjoy their feast.

CERATOSAURUS

ORDER: Saurischia
FAMILY: Ceratosauridae
PERIOD: Late Jurassic

HOME TERRITORY: USA, Portugal and possibly Africa
HABITAT: Swamps
SIZE: 6 m (20 ft) long

🔧 7	🦖 1	⚡ 5	☠️ 8	★ 4	⏱️ 6

DISTINGUISHING FEATURES

With strong jaws and dagger-like teeth, Ceratosaurus was a fierce, efficient hunter. Its short arms bore hands with four sharp-clawed fingers. It had a short horn on its nose, and bony crests above its eyes which gave it some protection.

DANGER 5.2 LEVEL

Like modern ruthless predators, the Ceratosauruses have picked on a smaller, weaker member of the herd to attack.

Ceratosaurus battle plan

This may not have been the biggest theropod in its habitat, but it was still a massive predator. Ceratosaurus was not just big, strong and equipped with a range of killer claws and teeth, it was a fast mover too. It could attack with speed and overcome its prey with deadly force.

BRACHIOSAURUS

ORDER: Saurischia
FAMILY: Brachiosauridae
PERIOD: Late Jurassic

HOME TERRITORY: North America, Africa, Portugal
HABITAT: Rivers and forests nearby
SIZE: 23 m (75 ft) long

🏋	9	🏃	0	⚡	2	☠	4	★	2	⏱	2

DISTINGUISHING FEATURES

This plant-eating giant weighed up to 45 tonnes. It had a long neck and front legs, so its body sloped down from the shoulders – and it could reach up into trees to eat leaves.

DANGER
3.2
LEVEL

Brachiosaurus battle plan

The mighty Brachiosaurus may have towered above most dinosaurs, but it had few other special skills on its side. Its battle plan was to go about its business and leave other dinosaurs alone, in the hope that they would not dare take on its mighty bulk.

TIME: Late Jurassic

THE BATTLE

WINNER: Ceratosaurus

WEAPONS OF WAR

Ceratosaurus

- Jaws lined with **dagger-like teeth** for ripping and gripping flesh.

- **Large, clawed hind-legs** were packed with muscles for speedy running.

- The front limbs were equipped with **long claws**.

- The size and shape of the tail suggests this animal may have been a good swimmer.

Brachiosaurus

- A **long, agile neck** meant that the beast could keep its important bits (brain, eyes, ears) away from a predator's teeth or claws.

- **Massive legs** the size of tree trunks were not vulnerable to attack.

- A **thick muscular tail** might have been used to whack predators.

- The shape of its head suggests this animal could **bellow loudly** – scaring predators away.

CRYOLOPHOSAURUS

THIS MIGHTY PREDATOR terrorized the plant-eaters of Jurassic Antarctica with its hook-like claws and jagged teeth. It was the first and only flesh-eating dinosaur ever found in Antarctica.

DANGER LEVEL 4.7

 7

STRENGTH: An immensely strong animal, Cryolophosaurus was able to overcome anything it attacked.

1

ARMOUR: Cryolophosaurus had no body armour but didn't really need it. Who would have dared attack this fearsome creature?

6

AGILITY: A powerful tail helped balance the weight of the front of this dinosaur's body, enabling it to run upright on two legs.

DISTINGUISHING FEATURES

Cryolophosaurus had a bulky body, powerful legs, and massive jaws. On its head was a crest with small horns which may have been used in mating displays.

Infraorder: Carnosauria
Family: Allosauridae
Period: Early Jurassic
Home territory: Antarctica
Habitat: Near rivers
Size: 6–8 m (19–26 ft) long

6

SCARINESS: This vicious hunter was the most frightening creature in its territory – the animal that all others did their best to avoid.

3

SPECIAL SKILLS: Like other large predators, this dinosaur hunted by stealth and speed. Having spotted its prey, it would wait for a chance to strike. When the moment came, this assassin made a dash to seize its prey.

5

SPEED: This dinosaur could run fast but only for short distances, so preferred to creep up on prey.

OPHTHALMOSAURUS

DANGER
4.3
LEVEL

A FAST SWIMMING HUNTER, Ophthalmosaurus belonged to the group of marine reptiles called ichthyosaurs. It cruised the seas of the world, preying on fish and squid.

4

STRENGTH: This ichthyosaur had powerful muscles and a strong body.

0

ARMOUR: Ophthalmosaurus had no body armour, but a thick layer of fatty blubber gave it some protection.

6

AGILITY: Like all ichthyosaurs, Ophthalmosaurus was an agile swimmer, using its paddle-shaped flippers to steer as it twisted and turned in pursuit of prey.

DISTINGUISHING FEATURES
This marine reptile had huge eyes, each the size of a human fist. It also gave birth to its young, instead of laying eggs.

Order: Ichthyosauria
Family: Ophthalmosauridae
Period: Late Jurassic
Home territory: Europe, western North America, South America

Habitat: The oceans
Size: 3.5 m (11 ft 6 in) long

3

SCARINESS: Ophthalmosaurus was an expert hunter of fish and squid. Although its teeth were small, it speed and size would have made it scary.

5

SPECIAL SKILLS: Thanks to its extra-large eyes, this reptile could see well in the dark and was able to track prey in deeper waters than other ichthyosaurs. It could stay underwater for up to 20 minutes between breaths.

8

SPEED: Ophthalmosaurus could speed through the sea at up to 40 km/h (25 mph). Its tail provided the main swimming power.

BATTLE TACTIC SPEED

For some of the smaller dinosaurs, speed was a vital tactic for catching prey. One of the secrets of the dinosaurs' success was that they moved more efficiently and more quickly than earlier reptiles. Creatures before them walked like most lizards do today, with their legs sprawled out to the sides. A dinosaur's legs were held straight down under the body, which meant they could carry more weight and take longer, faster strides. Many dinosaurs also used their tail to balance the weight of their bodies, allowing them to run on their hind legs.

BIRD-MIMIC DINOSAURS

Ornithomimosaurs ("bird-mimics") are known as ostrich dinosaurs. They were fast-running reptiles with beak-like mouths. It is possible that some ostrich dinosaurs could run faster than modern ostriches, reaching speeds of 80 km/h (50 mph). They were probably the fastest runners of all the dinosaurs. The ostrich dinosaurs thrived during the Late Cretaceous.

STRUTHIOMIMUS

This Struthiomimus's long slender leg bones kept the animal's weight down, so it was easier to run fast. Each foot had three claws. It probably used its clawed 'hands' to pick at food, such as berries and lizards. Its mouth was covered in tough horn to create a 'beak'.

ORNITHOMIMUS

This large reptile had very long, slender hind legs and powerful hip muscles – perfect for striding across the plains in search of all sorts of food. It ate juicy bugs, seeds and leaves, pecking at them with a toothless, beak-like mouth.

DROMAEOSAURUS

This swift reptile had huge eyes, which suggests it may have hunted in the dim light of dawn or dusk. It was not an ostrich dinosaur – it had long, toothed jaws. Dromaeosaurus could run and leap and belongs to the same family as Velociraptor.

A NEED FOR SPEED

Scientists work out how fast a dinosaur could run by examining fossils. They analyse the places where the muscles attached to bone and use this data to compare with modern animals. They can then calculate how the animal might have moved.

GALLIMIMUS

Like other ostrich dinosaurs, Gallimimus had a long neck and tiny head. As it ran, it probably lowered its head and raised its tail to provide balance, holding its clawed forelimbs close to its body.

BACK LEG OF GALLIMIMUS

Fast-running dinosaurs like Gallimimus had long, slender leg bones and slim feet. Big powerful thigh muscles allowed them to run fast and speed away from danger. This dinosaur was about twice the size of a modern ostrich.

Thighbone

Calf bones

Long, slender anklebones

Slim, three-toed foot

THE CRETACEOUS PERIOD

The Cretaceous period began 146 million years ago. During this time the climate was generally warm, but there were clear differences between the seasons. The first flowering plants evolved. Deciduous trees, such as oaks and magnolias, flowering bushes and herbs became more common than horsetails, cycads and ferns, and covered much of the land. More plants meant more food for dinosaurs, and many new kinds of dinosaurs, such as horned dinosaurs and duckbills, appeared. Pollinating insects evolved too, and more kinds of mammals and birds, many of which fed on plants and seeds. But the dinosaurs' days were numbered. At the end of the Cretaceous, some huge catastrophe on Earth, possibly the impact of a giant meteorite, led to the death of the dinosaurs and many other kinds of creatures, including pterosaurs and plesiosaurs. These amazing reptiles disappeared forever.

Pteranodon

Tyrannosaurus Rex

Gallimimus

DEINONYCHUS
— VS —
TENONTOSAURUS

It is a warm, muggy day and a group of Tenontosauruses are quietly grazing when three vicious predators leap out from the forest. A single Tenontosaurus is separated out by the pack of Deinonychuses. They are working together as they leap forward, holding down its body with their weight as their scythe-like claws dig in. The Deinonychuses begin to feed and the struggling Tenontosaurus takes its final breaths.

DEINONYCHUS

ORDER: Saurischia
FAMILY: Dromaeosauridae
PERIOD: Early Cretaceous

HOME TERRITORY: North America: Montana
HABITAT: Forests and swamps
SIZE: 3–4 m (10–13 ft) long

🔨 4	🦖 0	⚒ 7	☠ 7	★ 5	⏱ 7

DISTINGUISHING FEATURES
Fast-moving hunter Deinonychus had special weapons for attacking its prey. On the second toe of each foot was a large curved claw that the dinosaur could use to slash at its victim.

DANGER
5
LEVEL

Thrashing its tail from side to side is an effective defence, but the Tenontosaurus is being attacked on all sides.

Deinonychus battle plan

Like a modern day wolf or lion, this carnivore had a range to skills to rely on. It was probably quite clever and may have hunted in a pack. It was a fast mover and could pin its prey down using large, clawed feet. It may even have been warm-blooded which meant it could hunt in the cooler evenings, when most reptiles are sluggish.

WEAPONS OF WAR

Deinonychus

- On the second toe of each foot was a **large curved claw** for slashing.
- Powerful jaws were lined with **curved teeth, with serrated edges** like a steak knife.
- A **bite force** similar to that of a modern-day alligator meant it could bite through bone.

Tenontosaurus

- **Strong, clawed feet** for kicking and thrashing in self-defence.
- Its **large size** deterred hunters from picking on this beast as it grazed.
- A **horny beak-like mouth** could deliver a painful bite.

TENONTOSAURUS

ORDER: Ornithischia
FAMILY: Tenontosauridae
PERIOD: Early Cretaceous

HOME TERRITORY: North America
HABITAT: Forests and swamps
SIZE: 7 m (22 ft)

🔨 6	🏃 0	⚡ 3	☠️ 3	★ 2	⏱️ 4

DISTINGUISHING FEATURES

This dinosaur probably walked on its hind legs, and balanced its body with an unusually long, wide tail. It was large and heavy for an Ornithschian.

DANGER
3
LEVEL

Tenontosaurus battle plan

Like other plant-eating dinosaurs, Tenontosaurus relied on its size to scare off predators. Battling this bulky body would have taken great strength, or pack power. Tenontosaurus remained on high alert while it grazed – looking, listening and sniffing the air to check for any signs of danger lurking nearby.

41

IGUANODON

DANGER
4.2
LEVEL

PLANT-EATING IGUANODON lived in herds, which roamed Cretaceous woodlands searching for food to eat. Iguanodon was only the second dinosaur to be discovered, back in the nineteenth century.

 8

STRENGTH: With it large, muscular body, Iguanodon was a strong dinosaur, capable of defending itself from enemies.

1

ARMOUR: Iguanodon had no body armour – except its thumb spikes.

2

AGILITY: Although too bulky to be very agile, Iguanodon could rear up on two legs to feed on high plants.

DISTINGUISHING FEATURES

Iguanodon was a big, bulky animal with strong legs and hoof-like nails on its feet. Its arms were shorter than its legs, but it generally walked on all fours. On each hand Iguanodon had a sharp spike instead of a thumb.

Order: Ornithischia
Family: Iguanodontidae
Period: Early Cretaceous
Home territory: Europe, North America
Habitat: Woodlands
Size: 9 m (30 ft) long

6

SCARINESS: A full-grown Iguanodon could weigh up to 7 tonnes, so was a daunting prospect for any predator.

5

SPECIAL SKILLS: If attacked, Iguanodon could use its thumb spike to defend itself, driving it into its attacker's flesh or eyes.

3

SPEED: This dinosaur generally moved slowly as it wandered from plant to plant, but could run at up to 30 km/h (20 mph) if threatened.

KRONOSAURUS

DANGER
6
LEVEL

THE TIGER OF THE SEA, this pliosaur was a ferocious underwater hunter and just as terrifying as the dinosaurs on land.

7

STRENGTH: This marine reptile was hugely strong, capable of overcoming most other sea creatures of the time.

0

ARMOUR: Kronosaurus had no body armour – but few creatures would have dared to attack this monster.

7

AGILITY: Kronosaurus was agile in the water, able to change direction with ease as it chased its prey. It could also drag itself along on land for short distances.

Order: Plesiosauria
Family: Pliosauridae
Period: Early Cretaceous
Home territory: Europe
Habitat: Australia
Size: 10 m (33 ft) long

DISTINGUISHING FEATURES

Kronosaurus was the biggest of the marine reptiles known as pliosaurs. These fierce creatures had huge heads and jaws lined with strong, sharp teeth, so they could catch bigger prey than other marine reptiles. Its long flippers helped power it through the water.

9

SCARINESS: This mighty-jawed predator was one of the most terrifying sights in Cretaceous seas.

7

SPECIAL SKILLS: Its strong teeth and jaws meant that Kronosaurus could prey on more or less anything it chose, including hard-shelled shellfish.

6

SPEED: A fast swimmer, Kronosaurus moved with the help of its four powerful flippers.

BATTLE TACTIC ARMOUR

SOME DINOSAURS RELIED on speed to protect them from danger. Many of the sauropods were just too big to be preyed on. For others, body armour was the best defence. If attacked, armoured dinosaurs could bellow, thrash and stamp – while the predator tried to find a way through the spikes, plates and studs. They often gave up!

BODY PLATES AND SPIKES

Dinosaurs such as the Stegosaurus, Ornithosuchus and Sauropelta protected their heavy bodies with tough plates, bony nodes and thick spikes to shield their skin. While the Stegosaurus lacked horns to protect their heads against attack, they possessed formidable weapons at the end of their tails in the form of 60centimetre (2 foot) long spikes.

STEGOSAURUS

The double row of pointed, bony plates on a Stegosaurus' back would certainly have put off many predators and made this stegosaur harder to attack. The plates also made the dinosaur look even larger than it really was.

SAUROPELTA

This dinosaur's massive body was covered in a strong, bony armour. Flexible, horn-covered plates ran over it from the neck to the end of the long, tapering tail. A row of sharp spikes stuck out from each side to protect Sauropelta from attack.

STYRACOSAURUS

This dinosaur had a massive nose horn as well as large spikes on its neck frill. If necessary, this dinosaur would lower its spiky head and charge towards its enemy. Most predators would want to get well out of the way of those horns.

HARD HEADS AND BONY CLUBS

Some armoured dinosaurs like the Talarurus, Ankylosaurus and Euoplocephalus defended themselves with bony clubs at the end of their tails. Others, such as the Homalocephale and Pachycephalosaurus, had remarkably tough bony heads with horned ridges to protect them.

PACHYCEPHALOSAURUS

The heavy, 60 centimetre (2 foot) long skull of this bonehead dinosaur was 25 centimetres (10 inches) thick. It acted as a crash helmet, protecting it against attackers, or rival males in a contest for females. It may have rammed the side of its opponents, rather than its head — which was less likely to cause damage to itself.

EUOPLOCEPHALUS

The Euoplocephalus was doubly protected with its clubbed tail and heavy armour. Even the eyelids were protected. Pieces of bone came down like shutters over the normal lids to protect the dinosaur's eyes from sharp claws.

PACHYCEPHALOSAURUS
— VS —
PACHYCEPHALOSAURUS

Pachycephalosauruses belonged to a group of dinosaurs known as boneheads. Their skulls grew up to 25 centimetres (10 inches) thick.

THESE PLANT-EATING DINOSAURS lead peaceful lives most of the time — but it's mating season and males are pumped up and ready to fight. These two love rivals have a simple head-butting strategy — it's head down, charge and may the best beast win!

TIME: Late Cretaceous

THE BATTLE

WINNER: Pachycephalosaurus

WEAPONS OF WAR
Pachycephalosaurus

- **Thickened bone** in the skull protected the small brain during a head-butting session.

- **Lumps, bumps and bony spikes** on the skull would deflect heavy blows to the head and cause more damage to an opponent.

- **Strong backbones and solid legs** helped the dinosaurs to stand their ground when under attack.

- **Strong, short necks** could withstand the force of an attack.

- A **thick muscular tail** kept the animal balanced as it charged.

Pachycephalosaurus battle plan

When charging an enemy, whether a rival male or a predator, Pachycephalosaurus held its head down and its tail straight out, then ran as fast as it could to ram its bony skull into its opponent. It may have rammed the enemy's side rather than its head – which was less likely to cause damage to itself.

PACHYCEPHALOSAURUS

ORDER: Ornithischia
FAMILY: Pachycephalosauridae
PERIOD: Late Cretaceous
HOME TERRITORY: North America
HABITAT: Forests
SIZE: 4 m (15 ft) long

8 | 4 | 4 | 3 | 7 | 4

DISTINGUISHING FEATURES
The biggest of the bonehead dinosaurs, Pachycephalosaurus had a beefy body and long, heavy tail. Its back legs were sturdy and strong, but its front legs were extremely short.

DANGER
5
LEVEL

CARNOTAURUS

THIS DINOSAUR'S NAME means "meat-eating bull", and its horns certainly give it a bull-like appearance. Carnotaurus was one of the largest, fiercest hunters in Cretaceous South America.

7

STRENGTH: This massive hunter weighed as much as a tonne and had a powerful, muscular body. But despite the size of its head, its jaws were surprisingly weak.

7

ARMOUR: Carnotaurus's body was covered with small cone-shaped spines, which would have helped protect it from the claws of struggling prey.

7

AGILITY: Long back legs made this large creature surprisingly agile, able to jump with ease as it ambushed prey.

DISTINGUISHING FEATURES

This unusual theropod had strange little horns above its eyes, like wing-shaped eyebrows. Its eyes faced partly forwards.

Order: Saurischia
Family: Abelisauridae
Period: Mid to Late Cretaceous
Home territory: South America: Argentina
Habitat: Plains
Size: 7.5 m (24 ft 6 in) long

8

SCARINESS: Not held back by its tiny arms, Carnotaurus was an awe-inspiring predator and would have terrified most sensible creatures of the time.

7

SPECIAL SKILLS: Carnotaurus could have used its tough horns in head-butting contests with rivals as well as for attacking prey.

7

SPEED: A long, straight tail counter-balanced an unusually thick neck. Both features suggest this beast was a fast runner.

BARYONYX

DANGER
5.3
LEVEL

BARYONYX WAS a large dinosaur that lived on a diet of fish. Its long mouth was ideally shaped for grabbing slippery prey from a river's shallows, just like a modern crocodile.

5

STRENGTH: Like all big dinosaurs, this was a strong animal, but it didn't need great strength to capture its prey of small fish, and perhaps small reptiles.

1

ARMOUR: Baryonyx would have had a thick, reptilian skin but it had no horny plates or thickened scales to protect it.

5

AGILITY: This animal may not have needed to race around a river to find its prey, but it did need to be able to twist its neck and dive its head underwater to catch fish.

DISTINGUISHING FEATURES
Most meat-eating dinosaurs had tall, round snouts but the snout of Baryonyx was long, low and spoon-shaped at the end. Its teeth were also different to those of most meat-eating dinosaurs.

Order: Saurischia
Family: Spinosauridae
Period: Early Cretaceous
Home territory: England
Habitat: Along rivers
Size: 9.5 m (31 ft) long

8

SCARINESS: The claw on each of a Baryonyx's front limbs was huge, curved and grew to an incredible 30 centimetres (1 foot). With these two weapons, this must have been a fearsome beast.

7

SPECIAL SKILLS: This hunter had tall, sharp and round teeth that were better for grabbing fish than cutting meat. Its teeth are similar to those of today's crocodiles and alligators.

6

SPEED: Fish-hunters need to be fast to spot and catch their prey. Baryonyx may not have been a fast runner, but it needed lightning-quick reactions if it wanted to fill its massive stomach.

BATTLE TACTIC AGILITY

Dinosaurs, just like animals today, needed to have every tactic at their disposal so they could catch prey or escape from danger. Many smaller meat-eaters depended on their agility, both to out-manoeuvre larger hunters and to get the better of prey. Creatures such as dromaeosaurs were sprightly enough to leap onto huge plant-eaters and deliver vicious bites while avoiding lashing tails. Even tyrannosaurs, with their huge bulk, were able to duck and dive to escape the struggles of their victims. Peaceful plant-eaters had to be just as agile as the predators that pursued them in order to escape their clutches.

DROMAEOSAURUS

This dinosaur belongs to a group known as the 'running reptiles' or raptors. Slim, but packed with muscles in its long hind legs, a Dromaeosaurus was fleet of foot and able to twist and turn when pursuing its prey.

FAST REACTIONS

Animals can be agile without being super-fast. It helps if they can react quickly, so those with good senses can hear, smell or see danger and take appropriate action to avoid becoming someone else's meal.

ANKYLOSAURUS

Built like an armoured tank, Ankylosaurus was a slow, lumbering herbivore that plodded through the Late Cretaceous landscape. When threatened, however, it could stand its ground and wield a mighty weapon in the form of a bony club at the end of its tail. At up to 10 metres (33 feet) long, the biggest Ankylosaurus was a worthy foe of Tyrannosaurus.

ELASMOSAURUS

Elasmosaurus, a fast-moving marine hunter, was an expert swimmer and very agile in the water. When hunting speedy fish darting in all directions, it was vital for a marine reptile to be able to turn quickly and seize prey with a lightning lunge of its long neck.

ADAPTABLE AND AGILE

By the end of the late Cretaceous some dinosaur types had become highly evolved to combine strength and speed. They could walk on two legs, or four, and even sprint for long distances.

DEINONYCHUS

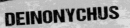

The darting Deinonychus was a nimble dinosaur that, like today's birds, was probably alert and fast-moving. It held its stiff tail out from its body – providing great balance as it twisted and turned – grabbing prey with its long claws and slashing at attackers with those powerful feet. This dinosaur lived during the Early Cretaceous.

CAMARASAURUS

The big, lumbering body of this sauropod was the opposite of agile, but that long neck gave it great freedom of movement. Sauropods typically had tiny heads and long necks – a combination that meant they could stand in one spot while reaching food all around them.

TYRANNOSAURUS
— VS —
TRICERATOPS

The huge body of a Tyrannosaurus must have contained massive muscles, giving it great strength.

WITH HUGE HORNS and a neck shield, Triceratops is a daunting enemy, even for Tyrannosaurus. But this monster is hungry so he ambushes his prey, sinking his mega-sized teeth into the horned dinosaur's side. Triceratops is bleeding but turns, wielding her horns and plunging them into the Tyrannosaurus. The wounded attacker retreats and rests to gather his energy for the final, fatal stages of the battle.

TRICERATOPS

ORDER: Ornithischia
FAMILY: Ceratopsidae
PERIOD: Late Cretaceous

HOME TERRITORY: North America
HABITAT: Woodland
SIZE: 9 m (30 ft) long

🏋 9	🏃 10	⚡ 4	☠ 8	★ 8	⏱ 2

DISTINGUISHING FEATURES
This colossal creature had a bulky body, heavy, pillar-like legs and a short, bony neck frill. Like all horned dinosaurs, it had a strong beak at the front of its jaws.

DANGER
6.8
LEVEL

Triceratops battle plan

Triceratops would stand its ground against a predator. If the hunter came too near, Triceratops would lower its head and charge, holding its huge horns at the ready to pierce the enemy's flesh. Triceratops was too heavy to rear up on two legs, but was able to manoeuvre its hulking head against an attacker.

TYRANNOSAURUS

ORDER: Saurischia
FAMILY: Tyrannosauridae
PERIOD: Late Cretaceous

HOME TERRITORY: North America
HABITAT: Most lowland areas
SIZE: Up to 13 m (43 ft) long

🔨 10	🦕 4	⚡ 8	☠️ 10	⭐ 10	⏱️ 6

DISTINGUISHING FEATURES

Tyrannosaurus stood up to 6 metres (20 feet) tall.
It had strong jaws lined with jagged teeth up to
25 centimetres (9 inches) long. Scientists think it
may have had a covering of feathers.

DANGER LEVEL 8

Tyrannosaurus battle plan

Tyrannosauruses were
Triceratops's main enemies,
but even they were wary and
stalked this monster very
carefully. Their best chance was
to attack a Triceratops that was
already wounded after a battle
with a rival male in the
breeding season.

WEAPONS OF WAR

Triceratops

- Two rows of **tough plates** ran down its back for protection.

- Long, bony tail spikes that could **slash a predator's skin**.

- A **flexible tail** that could move quickly with great power to deliver a blow.

Tyrannosaurus

- Dozens of very **large, serrated teeth** used like a hatchet to hack into prey.

- The ability to **open its jaw extra wide** to bite and devour prey.

- Powerful front legs, equipped with **long, sharp claws**.

QUETZALCOATLUS

PROBABLY THE BIGGEST flying creature that has ever lived, Quetzalcoatlus was also one of the last pterosaurs to evolve. This giant lived right up to the end of the Cretaceous.

7

STRENGTH: A pterosaur this size needed very powerful muscles to beat its mighty wings.

0

ARMOUR: Quetzalcoatlus had no body armour. In the air it had no enemies, but on the ground it was vulnerable to attack.

9

AGILITY: Like most pterosaurs, Quetzalcoatlus was very agile in the air and could swoop down to grab prey from land or sea.

DISTINGUISHING FEATURES

This huge pterosaur had vast wings, but its body was small and lightly built. It had a long neck and long, slender, toothless jaws.

Order: Pterosauria
Family: Azhdarchidae
Period: Late Cretaceous
Home territory: North America
Habitat: Marshland
Size: 12 m (39 ft) from wingtip to wingtip

7

SCARINESS: Size alone made this pterosaur an awe-inspiring sight. It also had a tough horn-rimmed 'beak' and small claws.

7

SPECIAL SKILLS: As well as scooping up prey from the sea or marshland, Quetzalcoatlus may have used its long, slender jaws to tear flesh from the bodies of dead animals, rather like vultures today.

8

SPEED: Quetzalcoatlus was a fast flier and an expert glider, able to soar for miles with scarcely a beat of its wings.

VELOCIRAPTOR

DANGER
6.7
LEVEL

THIS FEROCIOUS little dinosaur's name means "speedy thief". It probably ate anything it could catch and often hunted in packs. Velociraptor certainly proved the rule that there's strength in numbers!

5

STRENGTH: This dinosaur was speedy rather than strong, but it was powerful enough to attack and kill prey.

0

ARMOUR: Velociraptor had no body armour so needed to keep well away from enemies.

9

AGILITY: Velociraptor was a very agile creature, able to leap up onto a larger animal's back to attack.

DISTINGUISHING FEATURES

Velociraptor was a lightly built dinosaur with long jaws and plenty of razor-sharp teeth. It may have had a feathery coat covering much of its body. On each foot it had an extra-large claw for attacking prey.

Order: Saurischia
Family: Dromaeosauridae
Period: Late Cretaceous
Home territory: Asia
Habitat: Desert
Size: 1.8 m (6 ft) long

9

SCARINESS: Velociraptors were small but often hunted in packs. Together, they were deadly opponents.

8

SPECIAL SKILLS: Fossils of Velociraptor's skull show that it had a large brain and so was probably more intelligent than many dinosaurs. It probably had good eyesight and excellent hearing – vital for a hunter.

9

SPEED: This long-legged hunter could race along at up to 50 km/h (30 mph) and overtake many other dinosaurs.

TOROSAURUS

THIS HUGE HORNED DINOSAUR lived in herds and spent most of its time quietly munching plants. With its massive horns and neck frill it was a daunting prospect for any predator.

 9

STRENGTH: Like all horned dinosaurs, Torosaurus was an enormously strong animal – it had to be to carry its own body armour around!

8

ARMOUR: As well as the neck frill, Torosaurus had two long, sharp horns above its eyes and a shorter horn on its nose, which helped it defend itself.

5

AGILITY: Despite its bulk, Torosaurus was quick to defend itself and use its horns against attackers.

DISTINGUISHING FEATURES

Torosaurus was one of the largest horned dinosaurs. For many years, its skull was said to be the biggest of any known land animal, but a Pentaceratops skull has now been found that is even bigger.

Order: Ornithiscia
Family: Ceratopsidae

Period: Late Cretaceous
Home territory: North America

Habitat: Forests
Size: 8 m (25 ft) long

7

SCARINESS: Already an awesome sight, Torosaurus had another trick up its sleeve. The two holes in its crest were filled with skin that flushed blood red when the animal was angry.

★ 6

SPECIAL SKILLS: If threatened, Torosaurus would stamp the ground with a mighty hoof and lower its huge horned head to warn off its attacker. This would have sent all but the most confident predators running for cover.

3

SPEED: Torosaurus was not the speediest dinosaur. It had the legs of a plodder, not a fast runner.

MOSASAURUS

MOSASAURS WERE GIANT MARINE LIZARDS that lived in all the world's oceans during the Late Cretaceous. Mosasaurus hoffmani was the probably the largest of the group.

8

STRENGTH: This giant reptile was a powerful animal with a very strong tail.

0

ARMOUR: Mosasaurus had no body armour, but an animal of this size didn't really need protection.

8

AGILITY: This reptile was agile, too, and steered with movements of its paddle-like legs.

Order: Squamata
Family: Mosasauridae
Period: Late Cretaceous
Home territory: Europe, North America, Africa, Australia, New Zealand
Habitat: The oceans
Size: 15 m (50 ft) long

DISTINGUISHING FEATURES
Mosasaurus had a long, streamlined body and four short paddle-like flippers. Its enormous jaws were up to 1.4 metres (4 feet, 6 inches) long and filled with sharp, curved teeth.

10

SCARINESS: With its vast jaws open wide, Mosasaurus would have been one of the most awe-inspiring sights in Cretaceous seas. And this monster would have been able to snap up almost anything that came its way.

7

SPECIAL SKILLS: Each of this mosasaur's cone-shaped teeth had lots of cutting edges, enabling it to chomp down on more or less any other creature in the sea.

8

SPEED: Like other mosasaurs, Mosasaurus was a fast swimmer able to power through the water at high speed as it pursued its prey.

SPECIAL SKILL HERDING

Many plant-eating animals today live in herds. Creatures such as zebra, deer, and antelope find that life is safer in a group, where there's always someone keeping an eye out for danger. It was just the same for plant-eating dinosaurs such as duckbills, sauropods, and horned dinosaurs. Together, the dinosaurs were safer from predators and they could warn one another of approaching hunters.

FOSSILIZED FOOTPRINTS

Remains of footprints, eggshells, fossilized dung, burrows, and scratch marks are called trace fossils. They help scientists understand how prehistoric animals lived. Footprints may show where a group of animals travelled, and their different sizes and ages.

SAFETY IN NUMBERS

Dinosaur experts know that many kinds of dinosaurs lived in herds from the fossilized footprints that have been found. In some places, large numbers of prints show that adult and young dinosaurs moved together. Some meat-eaters also found that living in groups was an advantage. Together, small predators such as dromaeosaurs could attack prey much larger than themselves.

TRICERATOPS

If a dangerous predator approached them, horned dinosaurs such as Triceratops would take extra care to defend their young. The older members would make a protective circle around the young and shake their huge horned heads at the hunter. At the sight of this, even a tyrannosaur would usually change its mind!

LIVING IN GROUPS

The evidence suggests that some dinosaurs lived, travelled and fed as a group, and maybe even worked together to protect the family group. Today, most reptiles live alone, although birds and mammals often live as families or groups.

PARASAUROLOPHUS

Like most plant-eaters today, duckbill dinosaurs had keen senses of sight, smell, and hearing. If a Parasaurolophus spotted a predator, it could make a loud honking noise, maybe amplified by the hollow crest on its head, to warn others in the herd and give them time to escape.

BRACHIOSAURUS

As a herd of dinosaurs travelled together in search of food, adults walked on the outside of the group and younger animals stayed in the center, where they were protected. Predators usually picked their victims from the edges of a herd.

GLOSSARY

Ammonite An extinct relative of today's octopus and squid. An ammonite was a soft-bodied animal with tentacles that lived inside a hard-coiled shell.

Amphibian A four-legged animal with a backbone that lays its eggs in water. A young amphibian passes through a stage as a swimming tadpole before becoming an adult that can live on land. Frogs, toads and newts are examples of amphibians today.

Ankylosaur A member of a group of armoured dinosaurs, with a heavy ball of bone like a club at the end of its tail.

Armoured dinosaur Armoured dinosaurs were covered with plates of bone and bony spikes which helped protect them from predators. There were two kinds of armoured dinosaurs – ankylosaurs and nodosaurs.

Euoplocephalus and Sauropelta were both armoured dinosaurs.

Boneheaded dinosaur A boneheaded dinosaur had an unusual dome-shaped skull. Inside was a solid lump of bone that acted like a crash helmet to protect the dinosaur's head in battles. Pachycephalosaurus was a boneheaded dinosaur.

Carnivore An animal that feeds on the flesh of other animals.

Cretaceous The period from 146 million to 65 million years ago.

Cycad A cone-bearing plant that lived before flowering plants. A cycad had a short thick trunk and long palm-like leaves.

Duckbill dinosaur A duckbill was a plant-eating dinosaur with a long, flattened beak at the front of its jaws. The dinosaur used this beak for uprooting and gathering plants. Tsintaosaurus and Parasaurolophus were both duckbill dinosaurs.

Extinction The dying out of a species of plant or animal.

Family A group of a related species. For example, all the iguanodonts, such as Iguanodon and Muttaburrasaurus, belong to the family Iguanodontidae. The name of a family usually ends in "–idae."

Fossil The remains of an animal that have been preserved in rock. Hard body parts, such as bones and teeth, are more likely to form fossils than soft parts such as organs. Impressions in rocks, such as footprints, can also become fossilized.

Horned dinosaur A horned dinosaur had a large head with long, pointed horns. Most also had a huge sheet of bone called a frill at the back of their head that helped protect the dinosaur from predators. Triceratops and Chasmosaurus were both horned dinosaurs.

Jurassic The period from 200 million to 146 million years ago.

Mammal A four-legged animal with a backbone that has hair on its body and feeds its young on milk produced in its own body. Animals such as cats, horses, monkeys and humans are all mammals.

Nodosaur A member of a group of armoured dinosaurs, with long spikes sticking out to the sides of its body.

Order An order is a group of related families. There are two orders of dinosaurs – Ornithischia and Saurischia. The dinosaurs in the two orders differ in the structure of their hip bones.

Ornithischia One of the two orders of dinosaurs. All ornithischian dinosaurs were plant-eaters.

Paleozoic The era from 550 million to 250 million years ago.

Predator An animal that hunts and kills animals for food.

Prey An animal hunted by a predator.

Pterosaur A flying reptile that lived at the same time as the dinosaurs. Pterosaurs had wings made of skin attached to extra-long fingers on each hand. Examples of pterosaurs include Quetzalcoatlus and Rhamphorhynchus.

Reptile A four-legged animal with a backbone that has a dry skin and breathes air. Most reptiles lay eggs with tough leathery shells. These eggs hatch into young that look like small versions of their parents. Snakes, lizards and crocodiles are all examples of reptiles today.

Saurischia One of the two orders of dinosaurs. Saurischians included meat-eating and plant-eating dinosaurs.

Sauropod A huge, long-necked, plant-eating dinosaur. Sauropods were the largest known dinosaurs and included animals such as Diplodocus and Brachiosaurus.

Species A type of plant or animal. Members of the same species can mate and produce young that can themselves have young.

Triassic The period from 251 million to 200 million years ago.

Vertebra One of the bones that make up an animal's backbone.

INDEX

A

agility 7, 50–51
Allosaurus 24, 25, 26–27
amphibians 4
anapsid reptiles 4
Ankylosaurus 45, 50
Archaeopteryx 24
Archelon 4
archosaurs 12
Ardeosaurus 4
armoured dinosaurs 6, 7, 12, 18, 20, 21, 27, 31, 44–45, 50, 56
asteroids 7

B

Baryonyx 49
battle scenes 10–11, 16–17, 20–21, 26–27, 32–33, 40, 46–47, 52–53
"bird-hipped" dinosaurs see ornithiscians
birds 7, 12, 38, 59
bonehead dinosaurs 6, 46, 47
Brachiosaurus 6, 32–33, 59
brains 14, 47, 55
breeding season 46, 53

C

Camarasaurus 51
carnivores see meat-eaters
carnosaurs 6, 27
Carnotaurus 48
Ceratosaurus 32–33

Chixculub Crater 7
climate 5, 7, 8, 24, 38
Coelophysis 8, 20–21
coelurosaurs 6
conifers 8, 24
Cretaceous period 5, 38–59
crocodiles 4, 12, 49
Cryolophosaurus 34
cycads 8, 38
Cynognathus 10–11

D

deciduous trees 38
Deinonychus 40–41, 51
Desmatosuchus 18
Dicynodon 4
dinosaurs
earliest 5, 8
extinction 7, 38
groups 6
Diplodocus 25, 28
dromaeosaurs 6, 50, 58
Dromaeosaurus 37, 50
duckbilled dinosaurs 6, 38, 58, 59

E

eggs 30
Elasmosaurus 30, 51
Erythrosuchus 10–11
Eudimorphodon 9, 22
Euoplocephalus 45
Euparkeria 12
evolution 4, 7
extinction 5, 7, 38
eyesight 17, 22, 35, 37, 55

F

feathers 15, 53, 55
ferns 8, 24, 38
flowering plants 38
flying reptiles see pterosaurs
footprints 58
fossils
footprints 58
formation 5
        trace fossils 58

G

Gallimimus 37, 39
Gasosaurus 24
ginkgos 8, 24
Gondwana 5

H

hearing 11, 55
Henodus 31
herds 42, 56, 58–59
Herrerasaurus 16–17
hip bones 6
hoatzin 7
Homalocephale 45
horned dinosaurs 6, 34, 38, 45, 48, 52, 56, 58
horsetails 8, 38
Hylonomus 4

I

ichthyosaurs 4, 19, 30, 31, 35
Iguanodon 42
iguanodons 6, 42
insects 7, 38

J

Jurassic period 5, 24–37

K

Kentrosaurus 26–27
Komodo dragon 17
Kronosaurus 43

L

Laurasia 5
Liopleurodon 30
"lizard-hipped" dinosaurs see saurischians
lizards 4, 5, 6

M

mammal-like reptiles 4
mammals 5, 7, 38, 59
marine reptiles 4, 13, 19, 30–31, 35, 43, 51, 57
mating battles 45, 46–47, 53
meat-eaters 6, 12, 16–17, 20–21, 24, 26–27, 29, 32–34, 40, 48, 50, 52–55
Megalosaurus 24, 29
Mesozoic Era 5
meteorite 38
Microraptor 15
Morganucodon 8
Mosasaurus 57
Mosasaurus hoffmani 57
mososaurs 57

O

Ophthalmosaurus 35
ornithiscians 6
ornithomimids 6
ornithomimosaurs 36
Ornithomimus 36
Ornithosuchus 44
ostrich dinosaurs 36, 37

P

Pachycephalosaurus 45, 46–47
pack hunters 11, 20, 26, 32, 40, 55
Pangaea 5, 8
Parasaurolophus 59
Pentaceratops 56
Placerias 9
placodonts 13, 31
Placodus 13
plant-eaters 5, 6, 8, 18, 23, 24, 27, 28, 33, 41, 42, 50, 51, 56, 58, 59
Plateosaurus 9, 23
plesiosaurs 30, 31, 38
pliosaurs 30, 43
Postosuchus 20–21
prosauropods 6

Proterosuchus 8
Pteranodon 4, 15, 39
pterodactyloids 15
Pterodaustro 15
pterosaurs (flying reptiles) 4, 14–15, 22, 38, 54

Q

Quetzalcoatlus 54

R

raptors 50
reptiles
anapsid reptiles 4
early 4
flying see pterosaurs
mammal-like reptiles 4
marine 4, 13, 19, 30–31, 35, 43, 51, 57
rhamphorhynchoids 14
Rhamphorhynchus 14

S

saurischians 6
Sauropelta 44
sauropods 5, 6, 24, 26, 32, 44, 51, 58
Saurosuchus 16–17
Shonlsaurus 19
skeletons 15, 30, 31
skulls

26, 45, 46, 47, 55, 56
smell, sense of 10
sounds 33, 59
speed 7, 36–37
stegosaurs 6, 26, 27, 44
Stegosaurus 44
Stenopterygius 4
strength 7
Struthiomimus 36
Styracosaurus 45

T

Talarurus 45
teeth 10, 11, 12, 13, 16, 17, 19, 21, 22, 27, 29, 33, 41, 43, 49, 53, 55, 57
Teleosaurus 4
Tenontosaurus 40–41
therapsids 11
theropods 6, 32, 48
Torosaurus 56
trace fossils 58
Triassic period 5, 6, 8–23
Triceratops 52, 58
turtles 4, 30
tyrannosaurs 50, 58
Tyrannosaurus 52–53
Tyrannosaurus Rex 5, 39

V

Velociraptor 37, 55
vertebrates 14

W

warm-blooded 11, 40

CREDITS

Dorling Kindersley
12 Jon Hughes and Russell Gooday
15 Jon Hughes TL
18 Jon Hughes
19 Jon Hughes
37 Colin Keates C

Getty Images
36 De Agostini Picture Library TR

Shutterstock_
1 Michael Rosskothen
2-3 Kostyantyn Ivanyshen
4 Linda Bucklin
6 Ralf Juergen Kraft L, Catmando TR,
   3Dalia C,
7 Michael Rosskothen T, solarseven
   BL, Dariush M BC, Alucard2100 BR
14 Michael Rosskothen
15 Michael Rosskothen CL,
22 Leonello Calvetti
23 Linda Bucklin
24 Dariush M
25 Dariush M
28 Catmando
29 Michael Rosskothen
30 Ralf Juergen Kraft T, Lefteris
   Papaulakis C, Michael Rosskothen B
31 Michael Rosskothen C, Sombra BL,
34 Leonello Calvetti
42 Leonello Calvetti
44 ILeonello Calvetti T, Linda Bucklin B
45 Linda Bucklin T, Leonello Calvetti C,
   Ralf Juergen Kraft B
48 Catmando
50 Catmando
51 Bob Orsillo T, Michael Rosskothen
   C, Andreas Meyer B
54 Michael Rosskothen
55 Naz-3D
56 Linda Bucklin
58 Mark Higgins C
59 Catmando TL, TR, B
60 Michael Rosskothen
61 Leonello Calvetti
62 Catmando T, Michael Rosskothen B
63 Ralf Juergen Kraft
64 Marcio Jose Bastos Silva

Science Photo Library
50 Natural History Museum. London/
   Science Photo Library

Superstock
15 Universal Images Group / Universal
   Images Group BR
36 Science Photo Library/Science
   Photo Library BL
43 Stocktrek Images / Stocktrek
   Images
49 Stocktrek Images / Stocktrek
   Images
57 Stocktrek Images / Stocktrek
   Images

Battle scenes
8-9 various inc Jon Hughes and
   Russell Gooday Dorling Kindersley
10-11, 16-17, 20-21, 32-33, 40-41,
   52-53 Barry Croucher
26-27 Mick Posen
24–25, 38-39 Shutterstock
46- 47 Mark Turner
B=bottom, T=top, C=centre,
L=left, R= right